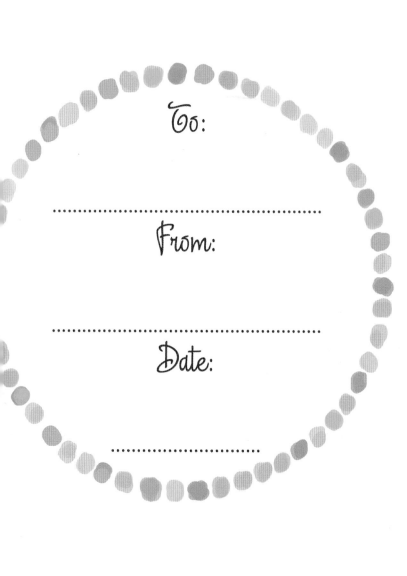

To:

....

From:

....

Date:

....

© 2012 by Barbour Publishing, Inc.

ISBN 978-1-61626-161-0

Compiled by Emily Garman in association with Snapdragon Group℠, Tulsa, OK.

All rights reserved. No part of this publication may be reproduced or transmitted for commercial purposes, except for brief quotations in printed reviews, without written permission of the publisher.

All scripture quotations, unless otherwise indicated, are taken from the HOLY BIBLE, NEW INTERNATIONAL VERSION®. NIV®. Copyright © 1973, 1978, 1984, 2011 by Biblica, Inc.™ Used by permission. All rights reserved worldwide.

Scripture quotations marked MSG are from THE MESSAGE. Copyright © by Eugene H. Peterson 1993, 1994, 1995, 1996, 2000, 2001, 2002. Used by permission of NavPress Publishing Group.

Scripture quotations marked NLT are taken from the Holy Bible, New Living Translation copyright © 1996, 2004, 2007 by Tyndale House Foundation. Used by permission of Tyndale House Publishers, Inc. Carol Stream, Illinois 60188, All rights reserved.

Scripture quotations marked NKJV are taken from the New King James Version®. Copyright © 1982 by Thomas Nelson, Inc. Used by permission. All rights reserved.

Cover and interior illustration: Shawn Banner, www.shawnbanner.com

Published by Barbour Publishing, Inc., P.O. Box 719, Uhrichsville, Ohio 44683, www.barbourbooks.com

Our mission is to publish and distribute inspirational products offering exceptional value and biblical encouragement to the masses.

Member of the
Evangelical Christian
Publishers Association

Printed in China.

Friendship: A to Z

An Inspiring Look at Friendship's Best Blessings

BARBOUR
PUBLISHING

How Do You Spell Friendship?

Forgive each other.

Refresh each other.

Invest in each other.

Encourage each other.

Nurture each other.

Depend on each other.

Share with each other.

Help each other.

Inspire each other.

Pray for each other.

Contents

Friends Are Kind and Understanding

Many a friendship—long, loyal,
and self-sacrificing—rested at first upon
no thicker a foundation than a kind word.

FREDERICK W. FABER

When we honestly ask ourselves which
person in our lives means the most to us,
we often find that it is those who,
instead of giving advice, solutions, or cures,
have chosen rather to share our pain and touch
our wounds with a warm and tender hand.

HENRI NOUWEN

The Heart of a Friend

Kindness and understanding manifests itself in numerous ways between friends. The unexpected meal at the most opportune time, a surprise card filled with encouragement, beautiful springtime flowers on the front porch. Each act of kindness leaves an indelible mark on a friend's heart. Each moment of understanding strengthens the cords that bind two friends together.

There's a reason we're encouraged to be kind and compassionate to one another. Although some acts of kindness may present an inconvenience or sacrifice of some sort, the rewards in the friendship are especially great because they are reciprocal. You are there for your friend, and your friend is there for you.

*Be kind and compassionate
to one another.*

EPHESIANS 4:32

Friendship is born at that moment
when one person says to another:
"What? You, too?
I thought I was the only one."

C. S. Lewis

12

Scatter seeds of kindness
everywhere you go;
Scatter bits of courtesy—
watch them grow and grow.
Gather buds of friendship;
Keep them till full-blown;
You will find more happiness
than you have ever known.

AMY R. RAABE

Nature has no love for solitude,
and always leans, as it were,
on some support; and the
sweetest support is found in
the most intimate friendship.

CICERO

Understanding friends will
always put the other person's needs
before their own. Instead of saying,
"Tend to me, tend to me!"
they are always saying,
"Let me tend to you."

Like everyone else I feel
the need of relations and
friendship, of affection,
of friendly intercourse,
and I am not made of stone
or iron, so I cannot miss these
things without feeling, as does
any other intelligent man,
a void and deep need. I tell you
this to let you know how much
good your visit has done me.

VINCENT VAN GOGH

The most I can do for my
friend is simply to be his friend.
I have no wealth to bestow
on him. If he knows that I am
happy in loving him,
he will want no other reward.
Is not friendship divine in this?

HENRY DAVID THOREAU

The key to friendship is being treated
with kindness, and respect lies in your
willingness to go first—
without expecting anything in return.

JOHN MAXWELL

The first and best expression
of love is kindness.

Friendship is the expressible comfort of feeling safe with a person, having neither to weigh thoughts nor measure words.

DINAH MARIA MULOCK CRAIK

One who knows how
to show and to accept
kindness will be a friend
better than any possession.

SOPHOCLES

A friend is someone who understands
your past, believes in your future,
and accepts you today just the way you are.

UNKNOWN

You measure a friend by the breadth of his understanding; I mean that delicate response from the chords of feeling, which is involuntary.

D. H. LAWRENCE

*The heartfelt counsel of
a friend is as sweet as
perfume and incense.*

P ROVERBS 27:9 N LT

Some of the greatest
surprises in life come when
friends show they really
know and understand you—
the perfect gift, or the card
with the perfect message,
or the perfect offering of help.

Kindness in words creates
confidence, kindness in thinking
creates profoundness,
kindness in giving creates love.

LAO TSE

Everyone hears what you say.
Friends listen to what you say.
Best friends listen to
what you don't say.

U N K N O W N

Love is patient and kind.
Love is not jealous or boastful
or proud or rude. It does not
demand its own way.

1 CORINTHIANS 13:4–5 NLT

Accept with gratitude
the companions God gives
you to go with you on the way.
Your task is to serve
and upbuild one another.

H. VAN DER LOOY

I always felt that the great high privilege, relief, and comfort of friendship was that one had to explain nothing.

KATHERINE MANSFIELD

30

Heavenly Father,
May my thoughts be kind and
my words and actions follow
after. May I bless my friends
with kindness and find new
friends to bless as well.
Amen.

A friend is one who knows you
and loves you just the same.

ELBERT HUBBARD

There is always a special kind
of freedom friends enjoy—
freedom to share innermost
thoughts and to show
their true feelings.

UNKNOWN

Friendships are glued together
with little kindnesses.

MERCIA TWEEDALE

Father,

I pray for those friends You've given me to walk alongside me, to encourage me, to love me. Show me how to serve and love these friends with Your love, as I should.

Amen.

Written with a pen.

Sealed with a kiss.

If you are my friend, please answer this:

Are we friends. Or are we not?

You told me once, but I forgot.

So tell me now, and tell me true.

So I can say. . ."I'm here for you."

Of all the friends I've ever met,

You're the one I won't forget.

And if I die before you do,

I'll go to heaven and wait for you.

UNKNOWN

True friendship isn't about being
there when it's convenient;
it's about being there when it's not.

UNKNOWN

Friends Stay True in Good Times and Bad

Friends are needed both for
joy and for sorrow.

YIDDISH PROVERB

Lots of people claim to be loyal and loving,
but where on earth can you find one?

PROVERBS 20:6 MSG

The Choice of Loyalty

At some time in our lives, we all will experience uncertainty, difficulty, or heartbreak. It's at those times the keen comfort of friendship is most often felt. In the throes of crisis, we know who in our circle are indeed true friends and who are not. In a sense, it is loyalty, rather than love, that carries the burden of proof.

Remembering who has been there for you in your hard times will increase your love and appreciation for those individuals. They are of great value. Cherish them and be sure to be there for them as they have been for you. Friends of convenience won't run to your side when trouble comes. Determine to have—and to be—a good friend.

A friend is someone who knows the song in your heart and can sing it back to you when you have forgotten the words.

UNKNOWN

When true friends meet in adverse hour,
'Tis like a sunbeam through a shower.
A watery way an instant seen,
The darkly closing clouds between.

SIR WALTER SCOTT

Don't walk in front of me,
I may not follow;
don't walk behind me,
I may not lead;
walk beside me,
and just be my friend.

ALBERT CAMUS

In prosperity, our friends
know us; in adversity,
we know our friends.

C HURTON C OLLINS

Friends love through all kinds of weather,
and families stick together in
all kinds of trouble.

PROVERBS 17:17 MSG

A true friend unbosoms freely,
advises justly, assists readily,
adventures boldly, takes all patiently,
defends courageously,
and continues a friend unchangeably.

WILLIAM PENN

You have blessed us, O God,
with the gift of friendship,
the bonding of persons in a circle
of love. We thank You for such a
blessing: for friends who love us,
who share our sorrows, who laugh
with us in celebration, who bear our
pain, who need us as we need them,
who weep as we weep, who hold
us when words fail, and who give us
the freedom to be ourselves.

Amen.

A faithful friend is a strong
protection; a man who has
found one has found a
treasure. A faithful friend is
beyond price, and his value
cannot be weighed.

BEN SIRA

You can always tell a true friend apart from an acquaintance based on their defense of you during a hard time. A true friend will stick up for and protect a friend no matter what.

It is a curious thing in human experience but to live through a period of stress and sorrow with another person creates a bond which nothing seems able to break.

ELEANOR ROOSEVELT

Friends come and friends go,
but a true friend
sticks by you like family.

PROVERBS 18:24 MSG

The friend in my adversity I shall always cherish most. I can better trust those who helped to relieve the gloom of my dark hours than those who are so ready to enjoy with me the sunshine of my prosperity.

ULYSSES S. GRANT

The firmest friendships
have been formed in mutual
adversity, as iron is most
strongly united by
the fiercest flame.

CHARLES CALEB COLTON

God, You know the good
times and the bad times
we will face in our lives.
You lead us down those
paths, but we are never alone.
You have promised to be
there every day, and You've
given us friends for comfort,
cheer, and fortitude.

Amen.

How strange that we should ordinarily feel compelled to hide our wounds when we are all wounded! Community (and friendship) requires the ability to expose our wounds and weaknesses to our fellow creatures. It also requires the ability to be affected by the wounds of others. . . . But even more important is the love that arises among us when we share, both ways, our woundedness.

M. SCOTT PECK

No matter how many times I go to
my friends with a problem, with a success,
with a request, I always find a listening
ear and a willing hand to serve me.
I could go to them thousands of times and
still find the same unfettered willingness.
There is great comfort in knowing
I have people in my corner.

Sometimes, with luck,
we find the kind of true friend,
male or female, that appears
only two or three times in a
lucky lifetime, one that will
winter us and summer us,
grieve, rejoice,
and travel with us.

BARBARA HOLLAND

A loyal friend laughs at your jokes when they're not so good and sympathizes with your problems when they're not so bad.

ARNOLD GLASGOW

Oath of Friendship

I want to be your friend forever

and ever without break or decay.

When the hills are all flat

and the rivers are all dry,

when it lightens and thunders in winter,

when it rains and snows in summer,

when heaven and earth mingle.

Not till then will I part from you.

UNKNOWN

Your friend is the (one) who knows
all about you and still likes you.

ELBERT HUBBARD

60

We were friends, and the warmest of friends, he and I,
Each glance was a language that broke from the heart,
No cloudlet swept over the realm of the sky,
And beneath it we swore that we never would part.
Our fingers were clasped with the clasp of a friend,
Each bosom rebounded with youthful delight,
We were foremost to honor and strong to defend,
And heaven, beholding, was charmed at the sight.

AMOTT LENNOX

Fidelity is an absolute
necessary in a true friend;
we can not rejoice in
men unless they will
stand faithful to us.

C. H. SPURGEON

Rejoice with those who rejoice,
and weep with those who weep.

ROMANS 12:15 NKJV

Man has only ten fingers—
just enough on which to count the
number of true friends one
can find in a lifetime.

UNKNOWN

It is so much easier to keep in touch with friends today than it was twenty years ago. All the more reason to stay involved with the ups and downs of our friends' lives. In this way, we can be true friends, even from a distance.

A true friend never gets in
your way unless you happen
to be going down.

ARNOLD H. GLASOW

Heavenly Father,

My friends are gifts from You.
You know how important they
are, and You've always been
faithful to provide friends
through every stage of my life.
Help me to be a true friend
to those You have sent me.
Show me how to give of
myself to them in good
times and bad.

Amen.

Friends Love Unconditionally

Friendship is love
with understanding.

ENGLISH PROVERB

Friends Love Unconditionally.
The greatest gift that you can give
to others is the gift of unconditional
love and acceptance.

BRIAN TRACY

Souls Bound Together

Soul mate. Soul friend. Soul sister. Soul brother. We attach those terms to people we love unconditionally, those forever friends. People we are attached to so strongly that absolutely nothing could tear us apart. They are our friends for a lifetime.

It's those belly laughing, affection-filled friendships that attach two people, heart and soul, with an everlasting love. That's the beauty of a soul friend—the unconditional love, devotion, patience, forgiveness, sacrifice. The connection between true friends is sometimes instant, oftentimes unexpected, occasionally memorable, but always with a deep permanence based first on affection, then love.

"I have loved you with an everlasting love;
I have drawn you with
unfailing kindness."

JEREMIAH 31:3

A true friend is someone who thinks that
you are a good egg even though he knows
that you are slightly cracked.

BERNARD MELTZER

If instead of a gem, or even a flower,
we should cast the gift of a loving thought into
the heart of a friend, that would be
giving as the angels give.

GEORGE MACDONALD

When twilight drops
her curtain down
And pins it with a star
Remember that you have a friend
Though she may wander far.

L. M. MONTGOMERY

Though our communication
wanes at times of absence,
I'm aware of a strength that
emanates in the background.

CLAUDETTE RENNER

"This is my commandment:
Love each other in the same way
I have loved you. There is no greater love
than to lay down one's life
for one's friends."

JOHN 15:12–13 NLT

A friend is one of the nicest things you can have, and one of the best things you can be.

DOUGLAS PAGELS

Friends will come and friends will go.

The seasons change and it will show,

I will age and so will you,

But our friendship stays,

strong and true.

U N K N O W N

I will pray for you, my friend.

I will name you in my heart before God.

If you are in trouble, or simply tired, I will do

all I can to lift your spirits. I will ache for you

in your sorrows and disasters and celebrate

with you in your joys and triumphs.

I will love and care for you always.

Friendship is the only cement that will ever hold the world together.

WOODROW WILSON

A true friend wants nothing more from you than the pleasure of your company.

UNKNOWN

A friendship can weather most
things and thrive in thin soil;
but it needs a little mulch of
letters and phone calls and
small, silly presents every
so often—just to save it
from drying out completely.

PAM BROWN

Heavenly Father,

Help me to be a good and true friend—to be always loyal and never let my friends down; never betray a confidence; always be ready to share everything I have; to be as true to my friends as I would wish them to be to me.

Amen.

I know I'm far from perfect.
I need my friends to remind me
of that lest my pride cloud the true vision
of myself. That's what it means to love
unconditionally. My friends are those who
will speak the truth in love at all times.
I need that in my life.

Don't just pretend to love others.
Really love them. Hate what is wrong.
Hold tightly to what is good.
Love each other with genuine
affection, and take delight
in honoring each other.

ROMANS 12:9–10 NLT

A friend is a hand that
is always holding yours,
no matter how close or far
apart you may be.
A friend is someone who is
always there and will always,
always care. A friend is a
feeling of forever in the heart.

C O L L I N   M C C A R T Y

To the world you might be one person, but to one person you might be the world.

A N O N Y M O U S

It takes a true friend to distinguish
our strengths and our weaknesses.
Someone who has spent time with us,
lived life with us, and cracked
the outer shell of our hearts.
A friend acknowledges all the parts
of our complex selves and
loves us still the same.

Few delights can equal the mere presence of someone we utterly trust.

GEORGE MACDONALD

There is no friend
like an old friend
Who has shared
our morning days,
No greeting like his welcome,
No homage like his praise.

OLIVER WENDELL HOLMES

Confidentiality is a virtue of
the loyal, as loyalty is the
virtue of faithfulness.

EDWIN LOUIS COLE

The glory of friendship is not
in the outstretched hand, nor the kindly
smile, nor the joy of companionship;
it is in the spiritual inspiration that comes
to one when he discovers that someone
else believes in him and
is willing to trust him.

RALPH WALDO EMERSON

You said, Lord, that You have
shown the perfect example of a friend.
Allow me to know You more and more
so that I may learn what it means
to be a true friend—one who loves
unconditionally and at all times.
Amen.

*I am very happy now
because I have complete
confidence in you.*

2 CORINTHIANS 7:16 NLT

A friend is one to whom
one can pour out all the
contents of one's heart,
chaff and grain together,
knowing that the gentlest
of hands will take and sift it,
keeping what is worth keeping,
and, with the breath of
kindness, blow the rest away.

ARABIAN PROVERB

No medicine is more valuable,

none more efficacious, none better

suited to the cure of all our temporal ills

than a friend to whom we may turn for

consolation in time of trouble,

and with whom we may share

our happiness in time of joy.

GEOFFREY CHAUCER

There are deep sorrows and killing cares in life, but the encouragement and love of friends were given us to make all difficulties bearable.

JOHN OLIVER HOBBES

The more we love,
the better we are,
and the greater our friendships
are, the dearer we are to God.

JEREMY TAYLOR

Friends Make Us Better People

Friends Make Us Better People.
My best friend is the one
who brings out the best in me.

HENRY FORD

She is clothed with strength and dignity;
she can laugh at the days to come.
She speaks with wisdom,
and faithful instruction is on her tongue.

PROVERBS 31:25–26

Make new friends, but keep the old;
Those are silver, these are gold.
New-made friendships, like new wine,
Age will mellow and refine.
Friendships that have stood the test
Time and change are surely best;
Brow may wrinkle, hair grow gray,
Friendship never knows decay.

JOSEPH PARRY

Friends are an aid to
the young, to guard them
from error; to the elderly,
to attend to their wants and
to supplement their failing
power of action; to those in
the prime of life, to assist them
to noble deeds.

ARISTOTLE

When friends, just by their presence in our lives, inspire us and uplift us and push us toward God, then we know what true friendship is.

Friendship is unnecessary,
like philosophy, like art. . . .
It has no survival value;
rather it is one of those things
that gives value to survival.

C. S. LEWIS

My friends have made the story of my life. In a thousand ways they have turned my limitations into beautiful privileges, and enabled me to walk serene and happy in the shadow cast by my deprivation.

HELEN KELLER

As iron sharpens iron,
so a friend sharpens a friend.

PROVERBS 27:17 NLT

Heavenly Father,
Thank You for placing friends
in my life who are by their
example, their words, and their
actions helping me to become
a better person. I am grateful
for each one.

Amen.

In everyone's life, at some time,
our inner fire goes out. It is then burst
into flame by an encounter with another
human being. We should all be
thankful for those people who
rekindle the inner spirit.

ALBERT SCHWEITZER

Today a man discovered gold and fame,
Another flew the stormy seas;
One found the germ of a disease.
But what high fates my path attend:
For I—today I found a friend.

HELEN BARKER PARKER

Friends are as companions on a journey, who ought to aid each other to persevere in the road to a happier life.

PYTHAGORAS

Friendship is a union of spirits,
a marriage of hearts,
and the bond thereof, virtue.

WILLIAM PENN

Close friends contribute to our personal growth. They also contribute to our personal pleasure, making the music sound sweeter, the wine taste richer, the laughter ring louder because they are there.

JUDITH VIORST

A friend can tell you things you don't want to tell yourself.

FRANCES WARD WELLER

To be a friend a man should
strive to lift people up,
not cast them down;
to encourage, not discourage;
to set an example that will be
an inspiration to others.

WILFRED PETERSON

Be the kind of friend that points others toward lofty goals and inspired challenges. In return, their successes will keep you on the road to ever-increasing excellence.

No man is the whole of himself;
his friends are the rest of him.

HARRY EMERSON FOSDICK

The more we love our friends,
the less we flatter them; it is by excusing
nothing that pure love shows itself.

MOLIÉRE

True friends don't sympathize
with your weakness—
they help summon
your strength.

U N K N O W N

A real friend warms you by his presence, trusts you with his secrets, and remembers you in his prayers.

UNKNOWN

God, I thank You for the gift
of friends who share life with me.
I am blessed to be a part of the
community You've given me.
May I never take it for granted.
Grant me the grace to reach out to
new friends and build the friendships
You've given me. May my life be
welcoming to all people.

Life is partly what we make it,
and partly what it is made by the
friends whom we choose.

TEHYI HSEIH

*Walk with the wise
and become wise.*

PROVERBS 13:20

If you approach each new person you meet in a spirit of adventure, you will find yourself endlessly fascinated by new channels of thought and experience and personality that you encounter.

ELEANOR ROOSEVELT

Friends are to be feared,
not so much for what they
make us do as for what
they keep us from doing.

HENRIK IBSEN

Friendship is essentially a partnership.

ARISTOTLE

No man is wise enough
by himself.

PLAUTUS

Friendship is a strong and
habitual inclination in two
persons to promote the
good and happiness
of one another.

EUSTACE BUDGELL

Friendship without self-interest is one of the rare and beautiful things in life.

JAMES FRANCES BYRNES

May the sun always shine
on your window pane.
May a rainbow be certain
to follow each rain.
May the hand of a friend
always be near you.
May God fill your heart
with gladness to cheer you.

IRISH BLESSING